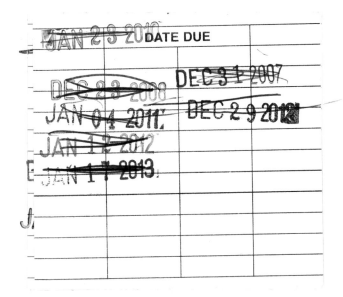

The Story of Christmas

by
VIVIAN FRENCH

illustrated by
JANE CHAPMAN

CANDLEWICK PRESS
CAMBRIDGE, MASSACHUSETTS

A long time ago God called for the angel Gabriel and gave him a very special message to deliver. God told Gabriel to go to a city called Nazareth and find the house where a young woman called Mary lived.

When Mary saw the angel, she was frightened, but Gabriel told her not to be afraid.

"God has sent me," he said. "God has chosen you to be the mother of His baby. He will be a wonderful baby, and his name will be Jesus."

Mary was surprised, but
she smiled at the angel.
"I'm happy to do whatever
God wants," she said.

Mary had promised to marry
a carpenter called Joseph. Joseph
heard that Mary was going to have
a baby, and he began to worry
about what he should do.

God knew that Joseph was worrying, so He sent an angel to visit him. When the angel arrived, Joseph was fast asleep, so the angel slipped into Joseph's dream.

"Don't worry any more," the angel told him. "This is God's baby, and when he is born you are to call him Jesus."

Mary and Joseph were waiting for the baby to be born when an order came from the emperor.

Everyone was to pay him some money. It didn't matter if they were old or ill or even if they were about to have a baby—the emperor said they must go at once to the city their family came from to make the payment.

Joseph's family came from
Bethlehem, so he and Mary had to
pack their things and leave Nazareth.
    As it was nearly time for the baby
to be born, they traveled very slowly
along the road to Bethlehem.

When Mary and Joseph reached Bethlehem, they found many other people there. Grandfathers and grandmothers, uncles and aunts, fathers and mothers, and sisters and brothers and cousins—everyone had come to pay the emperor the money he wanted.

All the places to stay were full.
Mary and Joseph knocked on
every door, but the answer was
always the same—no room, no
room. The only place they could
find was a stable, where the
animals were kept.

While they were there, the baby
Jesus was born. Mary wrapped him
carefully and laid him in a manger
full of soft hay.

The stable was not very far from some fields where shepherds were looking after their sheep. It was night-time, and very dark, but suddenly the sky lit up. High above them was an angel surrounded by light. The shepherds were very scared, but the angel told them not to be afraid.

He said, "I bring you the most wonderful news! Tonight in Bethlehem the savior of the world is born!" And he told the shepherds how they could find the baby, safely wrapped and lying in a manger.

Then, just as suddenly as the first angel had come, the whole sky was full of angels singing. They sang "Glory to God in the highest, and on earth peace and good will toward men."

When the angels had flown back into heaven, the shepherds rubbed their eyes.

"Let's go to Bethlehem!" they said. "Let's go at once!"

And they left their sheep and hurried off to look for the stable.

There they found Mary and Joseph, and the baby lying in the manger, just as the angel had said.

It wasn't only the shepherds who wanted to see the baby Jesus. A long way away three wise men saw a star in the eastern sky. They knew it was a sign that someone very important had been born, and they followed the star until it came to rest above the stable.

The wise men came inside and saw Jesus with his mother, Mary, and bowed down. They gave the baby presents of gold and sweet-smelling spices called frankincense and myrrh.

And up above the stable all the
angels sang as the star shone down.
The Son of God was born.

For Marcus and Sally
with love
V. F.
For George David
J. C.

Text copyright © 1999 by Vivian French
Illustrations copyright © 1999 by Jane Chapman

First edition 1999

Library of Congress Cataloging-in-Publication Data

French, Vivian.
The story of Christmas / Vivian French ; illustrated by Jane Chapman.
p. cm.
Summary: Retells the story of Mary and Joseph's trip into Bethlehem
and the birth of Jesus in a manger.
ISBN 0-7636-0762-2
1. Jesus Christ—Nativity—Juvenile literature. [1. Jesus Christ—Nativity.
2. Bible stories—N.T. 3. Christmas.]
1. Chapman, Jane, ill. II. Title.
BT315.2.F74   1998
232.92—dc21   98-22984

2 4 6 8 10 9 7 5 3 1

Printed in Hong Kong

This book was typeset in Calligraphic Bold.
The pictures were done in acrylic paint.

Candlewick Press
2067 Massachusetts Avenue
Cambridge, Massachusetts 02140